# Sticker
# DRESS UP

Join top MeDoll models Olivia, Sophie and Chloe, as they take part in catwalk shows and photo shoots around the world! Style the gorgeous girls with the stickers from the centre of this book — you can use the clothes chosen for each shoot or show, or mix them up to create your own unique clothing combinations! So let's get sticker styling, Stardolls . . .

BANTAM BOOKS

# Stately home style

The three girls are about to get all gorgeous and glam for a sophisticated stately home photo shoot!

# Rockin' on the rink

When the three models are wrapped up warm and snug, they're sure to look super-cool on the ice!

# Pretty in Paris

Olivia and Chloe love to look oh-so chic in the city, and their Parisian photo shoot is bound to be très bon!

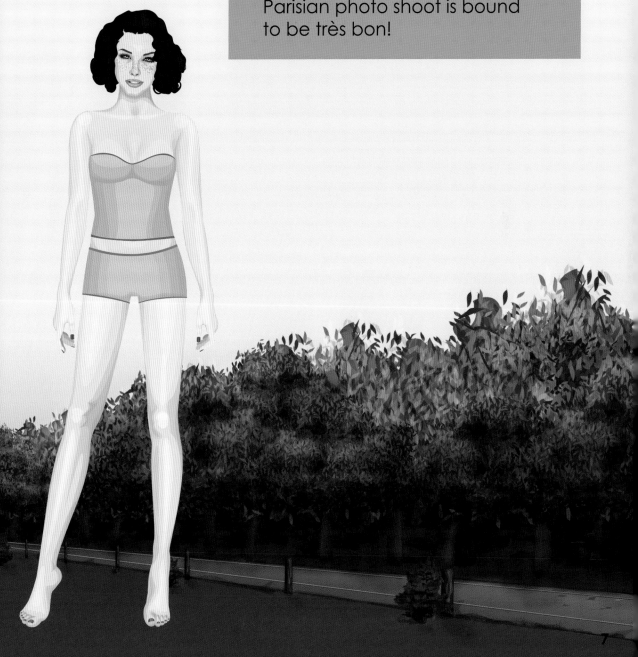

# Ballroom beauties

Chloe and her friends will be
the queens of the catwalk,
in their gorgeous gowns and
fabulous frocks!

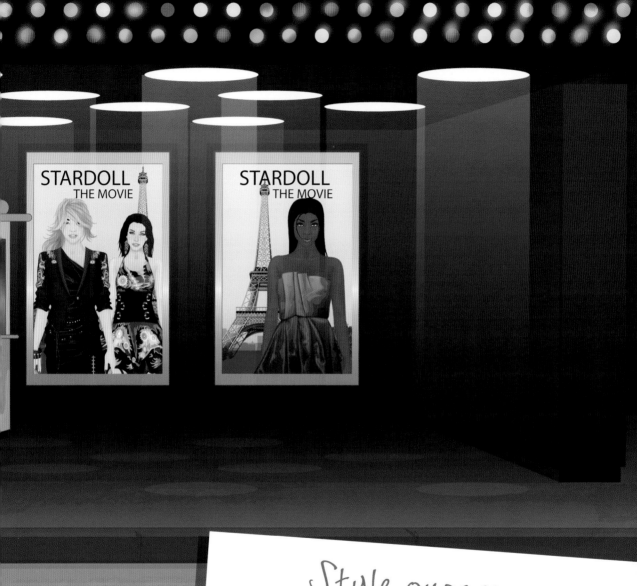

## Style onscreen

For such a dramatic and theatrical photo shoot, Sophie and Olivia require some truly show-stopping outfits!

# Dazzling divas

Olivia, Chloe and Sophie deserve to model dresses as dazzling as their surroundings for this photo shoot!

# Models in Marrakesh

The models will look amazing, when they parade wonderfully wild and colourful creations on the catwalk!

# Fashion flavours

In cute candy and ice cream colours, the girls look good enough to eat. This is a super-sweet photo shoot!

# Central Park poses

Central Park really is the perfect place for a photo shoot and the models are almost ready to get posing!

To collect your exclusive Stardoll gift, go to www.stardoll.com and login or create an account. Then go to the Gift Card section under My Account and enter this code, before 31/08/2013: RH-MTXLV2UKS

# Big top trends

With fun and flamboyant fashions, Olivia and Sophie can't wait to start this colourful, circus-themed photo shoot!

# New York, New York!

The girls are ready to showcase some outfits and strut their stuff on the catwalk at NY Fashion week!

We hope you have lots of fun joining in the Stardoll world.
Remember to be safe online and never give out your Stardoll password,
email addresses, or any other personal information, including photos.

STARDOLL: STICKER DRESS UP
A BANTAM BOOK 978 0 857 51124 9

First published in Great Britain by Bantam,
an imprint of Random House Children's Books
A Random House Group Company.

This edition published 2012

1 3 5 7 9 10 8 6 4 2

Bantam Books are published by Random House Children's Books,
61–63 Uxbridge Road, London W5 5SA

www.kidsatrandomhouse.co.uk
www.totallyrandombooks.co.uk
www.randomhouse.co.uk

Addresses for companies within The Random House Group Limited can be found at:
www.randomhouse.co.uk/offices.htm

THE RANDOM HOUSE GROUP Limited Reg. No. 954009

A CIP catalogue record for this book is available from the British Library.

Printed in Italy